Lao Zi's Dao De Jing
老子之　道 德 經

The Way of Nature
and
The Way of People

Chinese-English

First Edition

Dr. Auke Schade

nemonik-thinking.org

Copyright

First Edition

Published August 20, 2016

@ nemonik-thinking.org

ISBN 978-0-473-36988-0

Abstract

This book contains unique Chinese and English versions of Lao Zi's *Dao De Jing*, which means—*The Way of Nature and the Way of People*.

Lao Zi was a Chinese philosopher who lived during the 6th century BC but is still ahead of our time. His brilliance outshines intellectual giants such as Confucius, Sun Zi, Socrates, Plato, and Aristotle. Lao Zi's aim is achieving success, which is to *obtain what you seek and escape what you suffer*. Success is achieved by aligning the *Way of People* with the *Way of Nature*. Lao Zi's success is secular and based on competence, rather than devotion. It is about positioning, rather than competing. Lao Zi's deep understanding of nature and people is crucial for your immediate survival and that of the next generation. Humanity is facing overpopulation, dwindling resources, nuclear warfare, pollution, climate change, etc. We cannot solve those problems with the same way of thinking that is causing them. The brutal reality shows that our way of thinking is failing. Therefore, Lao Zi's eternal wisdom is the guiding light for our future. Its simplicity reaches peacefully across the boundaries of race, religion, spiritualism, ideology, and science.

Dr. Auke Schade

My life started during the devastation of World War II. As a teenager, I worked as a carpenter and studied building engineering at night school. During the seventies, I became a financial manager for a multinational corporation, ran my own business, and studied economics in my spare time. My interest in the psychology of management extended to the interaction between the mind, body, and reality. In 1980, I immigrated to New Zealand where I obtained a doctorate in psychology from the University of Auckland. My mission is to make people the smartest thinkers they can be, which has led me to the development of nemonik thinking.[1]

Download free eBooks and videos
@ nemonik-thinking.org

---

1 Appendix: Nemonik Thinking

Content

Notes

_____

_____

_____

_____

_____

_____

_____

_____

_____

_____

Introduction

Lao Zi (6th cent. BC) explains in one clear sentence the simple purpose of his allegedly mysterious *Dao De Jing*—*Use it to obtain what you seek and to escape what you suffer (62)*. His inspirational guideline provides a sophisticated yet simple principle for success.

Apparently, Lao Zi's biography was written down by the historian Ssu-ma Ch'ien (145-90 BC) who compiled the first comprehensive history of China. Nevertheless, mystery still surrounds the person of Lao Zi. Even his name is ambiguous. It could mean either *old boy* or *old father*. Some scholars suggest that Lao Zi was born with white hair and therefore was called *old boy*. On the other hand, *old father* might refer to a kind of honorary title such as *elder* or *old master*. Lao Zi's real name might have been Li Erh, who was a historian in the state of Chu.

Legend has it that Lao Zi left Chu because of the unbridled corruption in that state. Travelling through a narrow mountain pass, the keeper of that pass asked him to write down his wisdom. Allegedly, Lao Zi wrote *Dao De Jing* in one might. It might be that the pass refers to the change from life to death and that he wrote the manuscript during the last days of his life.

Dao De Jing might be a compilation of older ideas, because Lao Zi refers to the *Ancients* as his source of wisdom. However, we might say the same about any textbook of modern science. All those books show that in the past many scientists have contributed to the knowledge we have today. The only difference is that modern scientists have adopted the custom of mentioning the source of the ideas. Although honourable, that custom does not make knowledge any more reliable or valid.

The possibility that many scholars have contributed to *Dao De Jing* does not reduce the value of either the author or his manuscript. Although similar aphorisms might have been widely known at that time, *Dao De Jing* provides a consistent theory about the origin, formation, and working of the Universe. It is unlikely that such a sophisticated theory would appear accidentally from a compilation of unrelated sayings.

Dao means literally—*road, path, way, or pathway*. However, most scholars agree that in the context of Lao Zi's philosophy, *Dao* means—*The Way of Nature* or simply—*The Way*. The Way is the origin, principle, substance, and force of the Universe. On the other hand, *De* could be translated as— *The Way of People*. Furthermore, *Jing* denotes that scholars consider Lao Zi's manuscript a classic book. Thus, we could translate *Dao De Jing* as—*A Classic about the Way of Nature and the Way of People*.

It is hard to overestimate Lao Zi's wisdom and insight. He explains how to become a sage and use the inexhaustible forces of nature to your advantage. Sages are competent people who align with the *Way of Nature*. For that reason, they aim continuously to be in the right place, at the right time, with the right resources and in the right frame of mind.

Many wise people including Aristotle, Buddha, and Confucius have emphasized that moderation is the key to lasting success. However, only Lao Zi explains clearly why that is inevitably the case.

Right now, humanity's conventional way of thinking is failing, because it reinforces winning, rather than success. That leads to counterproductive criticism, rationalization, cognitive dissonance, and groupthink. As a result, we are facing manmade global problems such as overpopulation, dwindling resources, industrial pollution, insane warfare, and cold-hearted social-economic inequality. Yesterday's solutions have become today's problems. We cannot hope to solve those problems with the same way of thinking that has created them. Therefore, the eternal wisdom of Lao Zi's *Dao De Jing* is more relevant than ever.

Notes

Lao Zi's Dao De Jing
老子之　道 德 經

The Way of Nature
and
The Way of People

道

Dao

The Way of Nature

Chapters 1—37

1 The Way

道可道也非恒道也
名可名也非恒名也
无名万物之始也
有名万物之母也

故恒无欲也
以观其眇
恒有欲也
以观其嗷

此两者同出
异名同谓
玄之又玄
众眇之门

1

The Way that can be discussed is not the eternal Way.

The name that can be named is not the eternal name.

Nameless it is the origin of All-things.

Being named it is the Mother of All-things.

Therefore, be always without desire

and see the details.

Have always desires

and see the limits.

These two things occur together.

Different names with the same meaning.

Profoundly mysterious,

they are the gateway to many details.

2 Contrast

天下皆知美之为美也
斯恶已
皆知善之为善
斯不善已矣
故有无之
相生也

难易之相成也
长短之相刑也
高下之相盈也
音声之相和也
先后之相随恒也
是以圣人处无为之事
行不言之教

万物作而不始也
为而弗恃也
成功而弗居也
夫唯弗居也
是以弗去也

2

If everyone in the world recognises beauty as beautiful,

then there is already ugliness.

If everyone recognizes good as goodness,

then there is already badness.

Therefore, Existence and Non-existence

generate each other.

Difficult and easy turn into each other.

Long and short shape each other.

High and low fill each other.

Tone and voice harmonise each other.

Before and after follow each other forever.

Therefore, sages manage their affairs with Non-action.

They carry out their teachings without speaking.

All-things rise, but do not initiate them.

Act, but do not rely on it.

Succeed, but do not claim.

Only that what is not claimed

can therefore not be taken away.

3 Ruling

不上贤
使民不争
不贵难得之货
使民不为盗
不见可欲
使民心不乱

是以圣人之治也
虚其心
实其腹
弱其志
强其骨

恒使民
无知无欲也
使夫之知者不敢为而已也
为无为则无不治矣

3

Do not promote the knowledgeable
and the people will not strive.
Do not admire goods that are difficult to obtain
and the people will not steal.
Do not display what is desirable
and the people will not revolt.

Therefore, sages rule by
emptying the minds of people,
filling their stomachs,
weakening their ambitions,
and strengthening their bones.

Let the people be always
without knowledge and without desire.
Let those who know, not dare to act but stop.
Act with Non-action, then there will be no anarchy.

4 The Way

道冲
而用之有弗盈也
渊呵

似万物之宗
锉其兑
解其纷
和其光
同其尘

湛呵
似若存
吾不知其谁之子也
象帝之先

4

The Way is empty,

but use it and it has not to be refilled.

It is so deep!

Like the ancestor of All-things:

it smooths their blending,

untangles their disorder,

softens their glare,

and merges their dust.

Invisible.

Nevertheless, it seems to exist.

I do not know whose child it is,

but it seems to predate the Emperor.

5 Benevolence

天地不仁
以万物为刍狗
圣人不仁
以百姓为刍狗

天地之间
其犹橐籥与
虚而不淈
动而俞出

多闻数穷
不若守于中

5

The Sky and the Earth are not benevolent,
because All-things act as straw dogs.
Sages are not benevolent,
because common people act as straw dogs.

What is between the Sky and the Earth
is like a bagpipe.
It is empty, but not exhausted.
Use it and more will be produced.

Listening to many details is exhausting
and not as good as following your heart.

6 Valley Spirit

谷神不死
是谓玄牝
玄牝之门
是谓天地之根
绵绵其若存
用之不勤

6

The immortal Valley Spirit is called
the Mysterious Female.
The home of this Mysterious Female is called
the origin of the Sky and the Earth.
It seems to exist forever
and using it is no hard work.

7 Self-interest

天长地久
天地之所以能长且久者
以其不自生也
故能长生

是以圣人退其身
而身先
外其身
而身存

不以其无私欤
故能成其私

7

The Sky endures and the Earth last long.

Why do the Sky and the Earth last long and endure?

That is, because they do not foster themselves.

Therefore, they can live long.

Accordingly, sages withdraw themselves.

Yet they are first.

They put themselves outside.

Yet they are inside.

Because they are selfless,

therefore, their self-interest is fulfilled.

8 Goodness

上善
如水
水善利万物而不争
处众人之所恶
故几于道矣

居善地
心善渊
予善仁
言善信
正善治
事善能
动善时

夫唯不争
故无尤矣

8

Superior goodness is like water.

The goodness of water

benefits All-things and it does not strive.

It occupies places everybody dislikes.

Therefore, it is close to the Way.

In dwelling, the goodness is location.

In thinking, the goodness is depth.

In giving, the goodness is benevolence.

In speaking, the goodness is truth.

In ruling, the goodness is order.

In working, the goodness is skill.

In action, the goodness is timing.

Only those who do not strive

will therefore not fail.

9 Desire

持而盈之
不若其已

揣而锐之
不可长保之也
金玉盈室
莫之能守也

贵富而骄
自遗咎也
功遂
身退天之道也

9

Accumulating and filling up
is not as good as stopping in time.

Hammer it too sharp
and it cannot last long.
A room filled with gold and jade
cannot be defended competently.

Admiring wealth and arrogance
brings personal loss and misfortune.
When merit is achieved,
withdrawing yourself is the Way of nature.

10 Ruling

载营魄
抱一能毋离乎
专气至柔能如婴儿乎
修除玄
监能毋有疵乎

爱民治国
能毋以知乎
天门开阖能为雌乎
明白四达能毋以知乎

生之畜之
生而弗有
长而弗宰也
是谓玄德

10

Carry the 'corps de esprit'

and unite it inseparable with the One.

Concentrate vital energy and be as soft as an infant.

Study and eliminate mysteries.

Inspect them competently without flaws.

Love the people and rule the country

without using knowledge.

Open and close the gates of nature as a female.

Understand the surroundings without using knowledge.

Generate them and raise them.

Generate but do not possess.

Develop but do not exploit.

This is called profound virtue.

11 Non-existence

三十辐同一毂
当其无有车之用也
捻埴以为器
当其无有埴器之用也
凿户牖以为室
当其无有室之用也
故有之以为利
无之以为用

11

Thirty spokes merge into one hub,

but its Non-existence is useful for a carriage.

Moulded clay makes a cup,

but the Non-existence of clay is useful for a cup.

Chiselled doors and windows make a room,

but their Non-existence is useful for a room.

Therefore, using Existence is beneficial,

while using Non-existence is useful.

12 Ruling

五色使人目盲
五音使人之耳聋
五味使人之口爽

驰骋田猎
使人心发狂
难得之货
使人之行妨

是以圣人之治
为腹
而不为目
故去罢耳此

12

The five colours will blind people's eyes.
The five tones will deafen people's ears.
The five flavours will refresh people's mouth.

Galloping and hunting in the field
will overexcite people's minds.
Goods that are difficult to obtain
will harm people.

Therefore, sages will rule
for the stomach
and not for the eyes.
Therefore, reject that and accept this.

13 Favour

宠辱若惊
贵大患若身

何谓宠辱
若惊
宠之为下也
得之若惊
失之若惊
是谓宠
辱若惊

何谓贵大患
若身
吾所以有大患
者为吾有身也
及吾无身吾有何患乎

13

Favour and disgrace are just like distress.
They cause great suffering just like the body.

Why saying that favour and disgrace
are just like distress?
Favour is inferior.
Receiving it is like distress
and losing it is like distress.
Whether it is called favour or disgrace,
it is like distress.

Why saying that it cost great suffering
just like the body?
Why do I have great suffering?
That is, because I have a body.
If I had no body, how could I suffer?

故贵以身
于为天下
若可以寄于天下矣
爱以身
为天下者
可以寄天下矣

Therefore, those who purposely value their body
for serving the world
can be entrusted with the purpose of the world.
Those who purposely love their body
for the world
can be entrusted with the world.

14 The One

视之而弗见
名之曰微
听之而弗闻
名之曰希
搏之而弗得
名之曰微

此三者
不可致计
故混而为一
一者其上不谬
其下之不忽
寻寻呵

不可名也
复归于无物
是谓无状
之状无物之象
是谓惚恍
迎之而不见其首
随之而不见其后

14

Look at it, yet it cannot be seen.

Its name is called invisible.

Listen to it, yet it cannot be heard.

Its name is called inaudible.

Seize it, yet it cannot be caught.

Its name is called insubstantial.

These three phenomena

cannot be extensively evaluated,

because they merge into the One.

Above the One there is no void.

Below it there is no substance.

It is infinite.

It cannot be named.

Every time it returns to nothing.

It is called shapeless.

Like the shape of nothing.

It is called dim and elusive.

Face it, yet you do not see its head.

Follow it, yet you do not see its back.

执今之道
以御今之有
以知古始
是谓道纪

Adhere to the present Way
in order to manage the present Existence.
Use it to understand its ancient origin.
That is called the principle of the Way.

15 Ancients

古之
善为道者
微眇玄达
深不可识
夫唯不可识

15

Those Ancients

who practised the Way competently,

understood profoundly the smallest details.

Their depth cannot be known.

They cannot be understood.

故强为之容曰
与呵
其若冬涉川
犹呵
其如畏四邻
俨呵
其若客
涣呵
其若凌泽
沌呵
其若朴
旷呵
其若浴
涛呵
其若浊
浊以静之者将徐清
安以动之而者将徐生

葆此道者
不欲盈
夫唯不欲盈
是以能敝
不成

Therefore, they are difficult to describe and called:

"Careful,

like they were wading through a river in the winter.

Hesitant,

like they were afraid of their surrounding neighbours.

Solemn,

like they were guests.

Dissipating,

like they were melting snow.

Vague,

like they were simple.

Empty,

like they were a valley.

Merging,

like they were mud."

Do not stir mud and it will slowly clear.

If settled, stir it and then it will slowly come alive.

Those who keep the Way

do not desire fullness.

Only those who desire no fullness

are therefore able to exhaust themselves

without renewal.

16 Extremes

致虚极也
守静笃也

万物傍作
吾以观其复也
夫物耘耘
各复归于其根

归根曰静
静是谓复命
复命常也
知常明也
不知常妄
妄作凶

16

Concentrate on removing extremes.

Nurse tranquillity faithfully.

All-things around us rise,

and I watch them return.

Those things are numerous

and each one returns to its roots.

Returning to the roots is called tranquillity.

Tranquillity is called returning to order.

Returning to order is a constant.

Knowing this constant is brilliant.

Not acknowledging this constant is arrogant.

Arrogance causes misfortune.

知常容
容乃公
公乃王
王乃天
天乃道
道乃久
沕身不殆

Knowing this constant is embracing.

Embracing is honourable.

Honourable is Kingly.

Kingly is natural.

Natural is the Way.

The Way is forever.

It provides a content life without danger.

17 Ruling

大上下知有之
其次亲誉之
其次畏之
其次其下侮之

信不足
焉有不信
猷呵其贵言也
成功遂事
而百姓谓
我自然也

17

Great leaders are those known by their subjects to exist.

Next are those that are loved and praised.

Next are those that are feared.

Next are those low ones who are insulting.

If there is not enough trust,

then there is distrust.

Those of value speak about their plans

and succeed in completing their affairs.

Yet, the common people will say;

it happened naturally.

18 Ruling

故大道废
焉有仁义
知快出
焉有大伪
六亲不和
焉有畜兹
国家昏乱
焉有贞臣

18

Therefore, if the great Way is rejected,

then there will be benevolence and justice.

Knowledge and cleverness will appear

and then there is great hypocrisy.

Family relationships will be disharmonious

and then there is animal dirt everywhere.

The State's household will be a confused disorder

and then there is bureaucracy.

19 Ruling

绝圣弃知
而民利百倍
绝仁弃义
而民
复孝慈
绝巧弃利
盗贼无有

此三言也
以为文而未足也
故令之有所属
见素抱朴
少私而寡欲

19

Discard adoration and reject knowledge
and the people will benefit a hundred times.
Discard benevolence and reject righteousness
and the people will return to
filial piety and compassion.
Discard cleverness and reject profit
and there will be no burglars and thieves.

These three declarations
could be regarded to be inadequate slogans.
Therefore, let the people have also institutions.
Show modesty and embrace simplicity.
Lack selfishness and restrain desires.

20 Lao Zi

绝学无忧
唯之与诃
其相去几何
美与恶
其相去何若

人之所畏亦不可以不畏人
人望呵其未央哉
众人熙熙
若乡于大牢
而春登台

我泊兮未兆
若婴儿未咳
儽呵似无所归
众人有余
而我独若遗

20

Discard knowledge and there are no worries.
Flattery and rebuke:
how much do they differ from each other?
Satisfaction and dissatisfaction:
how much do they differ from each other?

What everybody fears, one has to fear as well.
Everybody stares at me. They do not stop.
Everybody is very happy.
Just like a big sacrificial feast in the village
and stepping on stage in the springtime.

I am quiet and not predictable.
Just like a baby that has not coughed yet.
Tired; without a place to return to.
Everybody has a surplus.
Yet, only I seem to be lacking.

我愚人之心也惷惷兮
俗人昭昭
我独若昏呵
俗人察察
我独闷闷呵

淡呵
其若海塱呵
其若无所止

众人皆有以
我独顽
以悝
吾欲独异于人
而贵食母

I am a very stupid fool in other people's minds.

Everybody is very clear.

Only I seem to be confused.

Everybody is very certain.

Only I seem to be very uncertain.

They are indifferent.

It is like staring at the sea.

It is like having no place to rest.

Everybody has a purpose.

Only I am stubborn

and my purpose seems to be ridiculous.

Only I desire to differ from other people

and value the food from the Mother.

21 The Way

孔德之容唯道是从

道之物
唯恍唯惚
惚呵恍呵
中有象呵
恍呵惚呵
中有物呵
幽呵冥呵
其中有精呵
其精什真
其中有信

自古及今
其名不去
以顺
众父
吾何以知
众父之然也
以此

21

The greatest virtue is following only the Way.

The contents of the Way
are only elusive and dim.
Dim. Elusive.
Inside there are images.
Elusive. Dim.
Inside there are things.
Tranquil. Obscure.
Its centre has energy.
Its energy is very real.
Inside it, there is information.

From past to present times,
its name was never erased.
Therefore, align with
the Father of the Multitude.
How do I know
that the Father of the multitude is like this?
From this account.

22 Sages

曲则全
枉则正
洼则盈
敝则新
少则得
多则惑

是以圣人执一
以为天下牧

不自见也
故明
不自视
故章
不自伐
故有功
弗矜
故能长
夫唯不争
故天下莫能与之争

22

Bend then be preserved.

Twist then be straightened.

Empty then be filled.

Exhaust then be renewed.

Lack then receive.

Have surplus then be confused.

Therefore, sages hold on to the One.

Accordingly, they are the shepherds of the world.

They do not display themselves.

Therefore, they are brilliant.

They do not regard themselves.

Therefore, they are honoured.

They do not boast about themselves.

Therefore, they have merit.

They are not arrogant.

Therefore, they will develop.

They do not strive.

Therefore, no one can strive with them.

古之所谓
曲则全者
几语也
才诚全归之

The ones called the 'Ancients' said:

"Those who bend will be preserved."

Is that saying insignificant?

However, true preservation was their return.

23 Align

希言自然
飘风不冬朝
暴雨不冬日

孰为此
天地
而弗能久
有兄人于乎

故从事而道者
同于道
从事于德者
同于德
从事于失者
同于失
同于德者
道亦德之
同于失
道亦失之

23

Speaking seldom is natural.

Violent storms do not drum all morning.

Violent rains do not drum all day.

Who serves them?

The Sky and the Earth.

Yet, they cannot go on forever.

So how about people?

Therefore, those who submit their affairs to the Way
will merge with the Way.

Those who submit their affairs to virtue
will merge with virtue.

Those who submit their affairs to loss
will merge with loss.

Those who merge with virtue
will also gain the Way.

Those who merge with loss
will also lose the Way.

24 Desire

跂者不立
自见者不明
自是者不章
自伐者无功
自矜者不长

其在道也曰
余食赘行
物或恶之
故有欲者
弗处也

24

Those who stand on tiptoe do not stand firm.

Those who display themselves are without brilliance.

Those who regard themselves are without honour.

Those who boast about themselves are without merit.

Those who are arrogant are without development.

Their Way is called:

"Leftover food and unnecessary action."

These things are disgusting.

Therefore, those who have desires

will not succeed.

25 The Way

有物昆成
先天地生
萧呵寥呵
独立而不改
可以为天地母
吾未知其名字之
曰道

吾强为之名
曰大
大曰逝
逝曰远
远曰反

故道大
天大
地大
王亦大

25

There was a thing undivided and complete
before the Sky and the Earth were born.
Desolate. Empty.
Independent and unchanging.
Yet, it acts as the origin of the world.
I do not know how its name is pronounced,
but I call it the Way.

If I were forced to name it,
then I would call it great.
Great means continuous.
Continuous means forever.
Forever means returning.

Therefore, the Way is great.
The Sky is great.
The Earth is great.
The King is also great.

国中有四大
而王居一
焉人法地
地法天
天法道
道法自然

Inside the Universe there are four Greatnesses
and the King is one.
Therefore, people follow the Earth,
the Earth follows the Sky,
the Sky follows the Way,
and the Way follows nature.

26 Attitude

重为轻根
静为趮君

是以君子终日行
不离其辎重
虽有环馆
燕处则
超然
若何万乘之主
而以身
轻于天下

轻则失本
趮则失君

26

Heaviness is the foundation of lightness.
Tranquillity is the sovereign of rashness.

Therefore, great men who travel all day
will not leave their heavy wagons.
Although, there is a walled guest house
in a quiet place nearby,
they remain aloof.
Just like a lord with ten thousand chariots
who considers himself
less important than the State.

Lightness will lose the foundation.
Rashness will lose the sovereign.

27 Competence

善行者
无辙迹
善言者
无瑕适
善数者
不用筹策
善闭者
无关籥
而不可启也
善结者
无绳约
而不可解也

是以圣人恒善救人
而无弃人
物无弃财
是谓袭明

27

Competent travellers
leave no trail.
Competent speakers
pursue no flaws.
Competent accountants
do not use bamboo counting sticks.
Competent wardens
lock without keys.
Yet, it cannot be opened.
Competent weavers
arrange without strings.
Yet, it cannot be untied.

Therefore, sages save people always competently
by not rejecting them.
Not rejected things are resources.
Accordingly, that is called brilliant.

故善人者
不善人之师
不善人
善人之资也
不贵其师
不爱其资
虽知乎
大迷
是谓眇要

Therefore, competent people
are the teachers of incompetent people.
Incompetent people
are the resources of competent people.
Those who do not value their teachers,
or do not love their resources,
although knowledgeable,
are greatly confused.
This is called the essential detail.

28 Contrast

知其雄守其雌
为天下溪
为天下溪
恒德不离
恒德不离
复归于婴儿

知其白守其黑
为天下式
为天下式
恒德不忒
恒德不忒
复归于无极

知其白守其辱
为天下浴
为天下浴
恒德乃足
恒德乃足
复归于朴

28

Know the male and guard the female
and become the stream of the world.
Be the stream of the world
and the eternal virtue never leaves.
If the eternal virtue never leaves,
then you will return to infancy.

Know the white and guard the black
and be the example for the world.
Be the example for the world
and the eternal virtue never errs.
If the eternal virtue never errs,
then it returns to moderation.

Know the pure and guard the disgrace
and be the valley of the world.
Be the valley of the world
and the eternal virtue will always be enough.
If the eternal virtue is always enough,
then you will return to simplicity.

朴散
则为器
圣人用之
则为官长
夫大制无割

Simplicity breaks up

and then it becomes tools.

Sages use them

and become official leaders.

They will not divide great organisations.

29 Desire

将欲取天下
而为之
吾见其不得已

天下神器也
非可为者也
为之者败之
执之者失之

物或行或隋
或热或坐
或强或赢
或培或堕

是以圣人
去什
去大
去诸

29

If anyone would desire to take the world

and interfere with it,

I see that they have no alternative.

The world is a container of energy

that cannot be interfered with.

Those who interfere will fail.

Those who hold will lose.

Things may succeed or may fail.

They may be hot or may be cold.

They may be strong or may be weak.

They may grow or may decay.

Therefore, sages

reject extremes,

reject grandeur,

and reject extravagance.

30 Force

以道佐人主者
不欲以兵强于天下
其事好还
师之所居
楚枌生之

善者
果而已矣
毋敢以取强焉
果而弗矜
果而弗伐
果而毋骄
果而毋得已
居是谓果而不强

物壮而老
是谓之不道
不道早已

30

Use the Way to assist the leaders of people.

Do not use soldiers to force the world.

Such actions are likely to rebound.

Where armies have camped

only thorny bushes will grow.

Those who are competent

succeed and stop in time.

Do not dare to take power.

Succeed without boasting.

Succeed without attacking.

Succeed without arrogance.

Succeed without excess.

That is called succeeding without force.

Strong things will become weak.

They are not called the Way.

What is not the Way will soon perish.

31 Armies

夫兵者不祥之器也
物或恶之
故有道者
弗居
君子居则贵左
用兵则贵右

兵者不祥之器也
故兵者非君子之器也
不得已而用之
铦袭为上
勿美也
若美之
是乐杀人也
夫乐杀人
不可以得志于天下矣

31

Armies are the tools of misfortune.

They are disgusting.

Therefore, those who possess the Way

will not claim them.

Great men will occupy and value the unorthodox.

They will use soldiers who value the orthodox.

Armies are the tools of misfortune.

Therefore, armies are not the tools of great men.

When there is no alternative then use them.

Attack with sharp weapons to become victorious,

but use them without satisfaction.

Those who are satisfied by it,

like to kill people.

Those who like to kill people

cannot achieve the goals of the State.

是以吉事
上左
丧事
上右

是以便将军
居左
而上将军
居右
言以丧礼居之也[2]

--- --- --- --- --- --- ---

杀人之
众以哀悲莅之
战胜
而以丧礼处之

---

[2] This line is divided in the English text.

Therefore, during fortunate events,
the left side is honoured.
During funerals,
the right side is honoured.

Therefore, junior generals
occupy the left side,
while senior generals
occupy the right side.
Their places are determined
in accord with funeral ceremonies.

If people were killed,
then many will attend with sadness.
Hence, treat battle victories
as funeral ceremonies.

32 Align

道恒无名
朴唯
而天下弗敢臣也

侯王若能守之
万物将自宾
天地
相合也
以降甘露
民莫之令
而自均焉

始制
有名
名亦既有
夫亦将知止
知止
所以不殆

32

The Way is forever nameless.

It is so simple.

Yet, the world should not dare to control it.

If Marquises and Kings would follow it,

then All-things would submit themselves.

If the Sky and the Earth

would unite with each other,

then it would rain sweet dew.

People would not have to be ordered,

but they would balance themselves.

If an organisation is established

names will appear.

If names appear,

then know that it is time to stop.

Know when to stop

and there will be no danger.

譬道之在天下也
犹川浴之
与江海也

The Way is to the world,

what a valley is to a river,

and what a river is to the sea.

33 Competence

知人者智也
自知者明也
胜人者有力也
自胜者强也
知足者富也
强行者有志也

不失其所者
久也
死而不忘者
寿也

33

Those who know other people are wise.

Those who know themselves are brilliant.

Those who overcome other people have power.

Those who overcome themselves are strong.

Those who know what is enough are rich.

Those who are strong pioneers have ambition.

Those who do not lose their institutions

will last long.

Those who die, but are not forgotten,

will live on.

34 Non-action

道溓呵
其可左右也
成功遂之事
而弗名有也

万物归焉
而弗为主
则恒无欲也
可名于小矣

万物归焉
而弗为主
可名于大矣

是以圣人能成大也
以其不为大也
故能成其大

34

The Way floats.

It can be unorthodox or orthodox.

It completes its affairs successfully.

Yet, it is not a famous being.

All-things return to it.

Yet, it does not act as their master.

It is always without desire.

Hence, it could be named small.

All-things return to it.

Yet, it does not act as their master.

Hence, it could be named great.

Therefore, sages can achieve greatness,

because they do not act great.

Therefore, they can achieve greatness.

35 Inexhaustible

执大象
天下往
往而不
害平大

乐与饵过客止
故道之出言也
曰淡呵其无味也

视之不足见也
听之不足闻也
用之不可既也

35

Hold on to the great image,

and the world will come.

It will come without

harm and with great calm.

Music and food will stop passing travellers.

However, words describing the Way

are called: bland and without taste.

Look at it, and there is not enough to see.

Listen to it, and there is not enough to hear.

However, use it and it cannot be depleted.

36 Action

将欲翕之
必古张之
将欲弱之
必古强之
将欲去之
必古与之
将欲夺之
必古予之
是谓微明

柔弱
胜强
鱼不可
脱于渊
邦之利器
不可以示人

36

To fold something,

it must have been unfolded before.

To weaken something,

it must have been strengthened before.

To abandon something,

it must have been attached before.

To seize something,

it must have been separated before.

This is called profound brilliance.

The soft and weak

will overcome the strong.

A fish should not

leave the deep water.

The sharp weapons of the State

should not be used in view of the people.

37 Simplicity

道恒无名也
侯王若能守之
而万物将自化
化而欲作
吾将镇之
以无名之朴
镇之
以无名之朴
夫将不辱

不辱以静
天地将自正

37

The Way is forever nameless.

If Marquises and Kings could follow it,

then All-things would transform themselves.

If this transformation would cause desire,

then I would suppress it

by using the simplicity of the nameless.

Suppressing it

by using the simplicity of the nameless

will not disgrace them.

Use tranquillity without disgrace

and the world will regulate itself.

Notes

徳

De

The Way of People

Chapters 38—81

38 Competence

上德不德
是以有德
下德不失德
是以无德

上德无为
而无以为也
上仁为之
而无以为也
上义为之
而有以为也
上礼为之
而莫之应也
则攘臂而乃之

故失道而后德
失德而后仁
失仁而后义
失义而后礼

38

Superior virtue pursues no virtue.

Therefore, it is virtue.

Inferior virtue pursues virtue.

Therefore, it is no virtue.

Superior virtue uses Non-action

and there is no action used.

Superior benevolence acts

and yet there is no use in those actions.

Superior justice acts

and there is purpose in those actions.

Superior propriety acts

and if there is no agreement,

then the arms are bared.

Therefore, after the Way is lost there will be virtue.

After virtue is lost, there will be benevolence.

After benevolence is lost, there will be justice.

After justice is lost, there will be propriety.

夫礼者
忠信之泊也
而乱之首也
前识者
道之华也
而愚之首也

是以大丈夫居其厚
而不居其泊
居其实
而不居其华
故去彼而取此

Those who have propriety
possess only a thin layer of loyalty and sincerity,
which is the beginning of disorder.
Those who pretend to know the future
are the fruitless flowers of the Way
and the chiefs of fools.

Therefore, great men occupy the thick
and do not occupy the thin.
Occupy the fruit,
but do not occupy the fruitless flowers.
Therefore, reject that and accept this.

39 The One

昔之得一者
天得一以清
地得一以宁
神得一以灵
浴得一以盈
侯王得一
而以为天下正

其至之一也
天毋已清
将恐裂
地毋已宁
将恐发
神毋已灵
将恐歇
谷毋已盈
将将恐竭
万物无以生

39

Of those in the past that obtained the One:

the Sky obtained the One through pureness;

the Earth obtained the One through quietness;

the mind obtained the One through effectiveness;

the valley obtained the One through filling;

and Marquises and Kings obtained the One

by regulating the world.

The conclusion about the One is:

if the Sky is not clear yet,

then fear that it will crack;

if the Earth is not quiet yet,

then fear that it will burst;

if the mind is not effective yet,

then fear that it will cease;

and if the valley is not full yet,

then fear that it will be dry.

All-things grow without purpose.

侯王
毋已贵以高
将恐蹶
故必贵
以贱为本
必高而以下为基

夫是以侯王
自谓孤寡不谷
此其以贱
之本与非也
故致数
誉无誉

是故不欲
琭琭若玉
落落若石

If Marquises and Kings

do not use superior nobility,

then fear that they will be overthrown.

Therefore, the noble

must use the ignoble as their foundation.

The high must use the low as their foundation.

Therefore, Marquises and Kings

call themselves unkindly 'orphans and widowers'.

They use that ignobility

incorrectly as their foundation.

Therefore, they give too much

honour without honour.

Hence, do not desire

the great splendour of jade,

but the grace of natural rock.

40 Non-existence

反也者道之动也
弱也者道之用也
天下之物生于有
有生于无

40

Returning is the movement of the Way.

Weakness is used by the Way.

The world's things originate from Existence.

Existence originates from Non-existence.

41 Attitude

上士闻道
勤而能行之
中士闻道
若存若亡
下士闻道
大笑之
弗大笑不足
以为道

是以建言有之曰
明道如昧
进道若退
夷道如类

上德如浴
大白如辱
广德如不足
建德如偷

41

If competent scholars hear about the Way,
then they are able to practise it constantly.
If mediocre scholars hear about the Way,
then they put it in a safe place and seem to lose it.
If incompetent scholars hear about the Way,
then they laugh loudly about it.
If they did not laugh loudly about it,
then they could practice the Way.

Therefore, an established saying states:
"The bright Way seems to be obscure,
the Way forward seems to be backwards,
and the smooth Way seems to be rough."

Superior virtue is just like a valley.
Great pureness seems to be disgrace.
Extensive virtue seems to be insufficient.
Established virtue seems to drift along.

质真若渝
大方无隅
大器晚成
大音希声
大象无形

道隐无名
夫唯道
善始
且善成

Plain truth seems to change;

the greatest square is without edges;

the greatest talent matures late;

the greatest sound is a rare tone;

and the greatest form is without shape.

The hidden Way is nameless.

Yet, only the Way

is good at the beginning

and good at the end.

42 Yin and Yang

道生一
一生二
二生三
三生万物

万物负阴
而抱阳
冲
气以为和

人之所恶
唯孤寡不谷
而王侯
以自名也

42

The Way generated the One.
The One generated the Two.
The Two generated the Three.
The Three generated All-things.

All-things carry Yin on their back
and carry Yang in their arms.
Their balance creates
vital energy that restores harmony.

People dislike being
unrelated orphans and widowers.
Yet, Kings and Marquises
use those names for themselves.

物或损之而益
或益之而损
故人之所教
议而教人
强梁者
不得其死
吾将以为
学父

Things may be harmed by benefit
and may benefit by being harmed.
Therefore, the teachers of humanity
discus and teach people
that violent people
will achieve nothing but death.
I will use that as
the father of my teachings.

43 Non-action

天下之至柔
驰骋天下之致坚
无有
入于无间

吾是以知
无为之有益也
不言之教
无为之益天下
希能及之矣

43

The softest of the world
will overcome the hardest of the world.
What is without substance
will penetrate what is without gaps.

Therefore, I know
that there is benefit in Non-action.
Teaching without speaking
and Non-action will benefit the whole world.
Only a few competent people can attain this.

44 Desire

名与身
孰亲
身与货
孰多
得与亡
孰病

什爱必大费
厚藏
必多亡
故知足
不辱
知止
不殆
可以长久

44

Fame or life?

What is closer?

Life or wealth?

What is worth more?

Gain or loss?

What hurts more?

Most people love to spend a lot.
The larger their hoard
the more they have to lose.
Therefore, know what is enough
and there will be no disgrace.
Know when to stop
and there will be no danger.
Accordingly, one will endure long.

45 Tranquillity

大成若缺
其用不币
大盈若冲
其用不穷

大直如屈
大巧如拙
大赢如绌

趮胜寒
静胜热
清静可以
为天下正

45

The greatest achievement seems to be incomplete.

Yet, its usefulness is not reduced.

The greatest fullness seems to be empty.

Yet, its usefulness is never exhausted.

The greatest straightness seems to bend.

The greatest skill seems clumsy.

The greatest triumph seems insufficient.

Activity overcomes the cold.

Tranquillity overcomes the heat.

Hence, pure tranquillity can be used

to regulate the world.

46 Desire

天下有道
却走马以粪
天下无道
戎马生于郊

罪莫大
于什欲
祸莫大
于不知足
咎莫憯
于欲得

故知足之为足
恒足矣

46

If the world possesses the Way,
then race horses will be kept for their manure.
If the world is without the Way,
then war horses will be bred in the suburbs.

No greater suffering
than having extreme desires.
No greater misfortune
than not knowing what is enough.
No misfortune is more disastrous
than the desire to accumulate.

Therefore, know that enough is enough
and there will be always enough.

47 Competence

不出于户
以知天下
不窥于牖
以知天道
其出也弥远
者其知弥少

是以圣人不行
而知
不见
而名
弗为
而成

47

Do not leave home

in order to learn about the world.

Do not look through the window

in order to learn about the Way of nature.

The more that people travel far away

the less they know.

Therefore, sages do not travel

and yet they know.

They do not see

and yet they name.

They do not act

and yet they achieve.

48 Non-action

为学者日益
为道者日损
损之又损
以至于无为
无为而无不为

取天下也
恒以无事
及其有事也
不足以取天下矣

48

Those who daily pursue knowledge will expand.

Those who daily pursue the Way will contract.

Contract and contract

until there is Non-action left.

There is Non-action and yet there is action.

If one wants to take the world,

then one should always use no effort.

When effort is needed,

then there is never enough to take the world.

49 Opinions

圣人无恒心
以百姓之心
为心

善者善之
不善者亦善之
得善也
信者信之
不信者亦信之
得信也

圣人之在天下也
歙歙焉为
天下浑心
百姓皆属其耳目焉
圣人皆咳之

49

Sages are always without opinions.

They use the opinions of common people

as their opinions.

They are good to those who are good.

They are also good to those who are bad.

So they gain goodness.

They trust those who trust them.

They also trust those who do not trust them.

So they gain trustworthiness.

Sages depend on the world.

Careful, so that they become

merged with the opinion of the world.

All common people focus their ears and eyes.

Instead, all sages are like children.

50 Competence

出生入死
生之徒十有三
死之徒十有三
而民之生生动皆之死地之十有三[3]

--- --- --- --- --- --- --- --- --- --- --- --- --- ---

夫何故也
以其生生也
盖闻善摄生者[4]

--- --- --- --- --- ---

---

[3] This line is divided in the English text.
[4] This line is divided in the English text.

50

Emerging into life is entering into death.

Three in ten are companions of life.

Three in ten are companions of death.

Three in ten people live extremely

and move into the realm of death.

What is the reason?

That is because they live extremely.

They are incompetent in

hiding, listening, and conserving their lives.

陵行不
遇兕虎
入军不
被甲兵

兕无所揣其角
虎无所措其爪
兵无所容其刃

夫何故也
以其无死地焉

Do not walk through the hills
in order to meet rhinoceroses and tigers.
Do not join the army
in order to carry weapons.

Rhinoceroses have no place to ram their horns.
Tigers have no place to strike their claws.
Soldiers have no place to thrust their swords.

What is the reason?
Because sages avoid the realm of death.

51 Competence

道生之
而德畜之
物刑之
而器成之
是以万物尊道
而贵德

道之尊也德之贵也
夫莫之爵也
而恒自然也

道生之畜之
长之遂之
亭之毒之
养之复之

生而弗有也
为而弗恃也
长而弗宰也
此之谓玄德

51

The Way generates them
and virtue raises them.
The environment shapes them
and competence completes them.
Therefore, All-things respect the Way
and admire virtue.

Respecting the Way and admiring virtue
is not done to obtain a noble position,
but it is always done to be natural.

The Way generates them and raises them.
It grows them and satisfies them.
It straightens them and matures them.
It supports them and repairs them.

Generate but do not possess.
Act but do not rely on it.
Grow but do not exploit.
This is called profound virtue.

52 Competence

天下有始
以为天下母
既得其母
以知其子
既知其子
复守其母
没身不殆

塞其兑闭其门
终身不勤
启其兑济其事
终身不救

见小曰明
守柔曰强
用其光复归其明
毋遗身央
是谓袭常

52

The beginning of the world
is the Mother of the world.
Obtain the Mother
in order to know her children.
When knowing her children,
return to their nursing Mother,
and life will not be in danger.

Block the exchange and close the doors;
and to the end of life there will be no hard work.
Open the exchange and meddle in affairs;
and to the end of life there will be no safety.

To perceive the small is called brilliant.
Following the soft is called strength.
Use its light to join its brilliance again.
Not losing life to disaster
is called following the constant.

53 Ruling

使我洁有知也
行于大道
唯施是畏

大道什夷
而民什好径
朝什除
田什芜
仓什虚

服文彩
带利剑厌饮食
而货财有余
是谓盗夸
盗夸非道也

53

Let me have pure knowledge.
When walking on the Great Road,
the only thing I fear is action.

The Great Road is very smooth.
Yet, people prefer the narrow winding roads.
Their palaces are very clean.
Their fields are overgrown with weeds.
Their storehouses are very empty.

Those who wear embroidered coloured silk,
carry sharp swords, gorge on food,
and have a surplus of goods and resources,
are called 'boasting thieves'.
Boasting thieves are not the Way.

54 Competence

善建者
不拔
善抱者
不脱
子孙以
祭祀不辍

修之于身
其德乃真
修之于家
其德有余
修之于乡
其德乃长
修之于国
其德乃丰
修之于天下
其德乃博

54

Those who establish it competently
cannot be pulled away.
Those who embrace it competently
cannot be separated.
Accordingly, descendants
will pay homage forever.

Cultivate it in yourself
and it will be genuine.
Cultivate it in your household
and it will be plenty.
Cultivate it in your village
and its virtue will last long.
Cultivate it in your country
and its virtue will be abundant.
Cultivate it in the world
and its virtue will be extensive.

以身观身
以家观家
以乡观乡
以邦观邦
以天下观天下

吾何以知天下之然哉
以此

Use yourself to examine yourself.

Use households to examine households.

Use villages to examine villages.

Use countries to examine countries.

Use the world to examine the world.

How do I know that the world is like this?

From this account.

55 Sages

含德之厚
者比于赤子也
蚖虺虫地弗螫
攫鸟弗搏
骨弱筋柔
而握固

未知
牝牡之合
而朘怒
精之至也
终日号
而不嚘
和之至也

知和曰常
知常曰明
益生曰祥
心使气曰强

55

Those who have substantial virtue
could be compared to new-born babies.
Scorpions, vipers, and insects do not bite them.
Birds of prey will not seize them.
Their bones are weak and their tendons soft.
Yet, their grip is firm.

They do not know
about the joining of male and female.
Yet, their male organ is vigorous.
Their energy is optimal.
They cry all day.
Yet, they do not become hoarse.
Their harmony is optimal.

Knowing harmony is called the constant.
Knowing the constant is called brilliance.
Benefiting life is called fortune.
Using the mind's vital energy is called powerful.

物壮则老
谓之不道
不道早已

Strong things will become weak.

They are not called the Way.

What is not the Way will perish soon.

56 Align

知者弗言也
言者弗知也
塞其兑闭其门

挫其锐
解其纷
和其光
同其尘

是谓玄同
故不可得而亲也
亦不可得而疏
不可得而利
亦不可得而害
不可得而贵
亦不可得而贱
故为天下贵

56

Those who know do not speak.

Those who speak do not know.

Block the exchange and close the doors.

File their sharpness.

Untangle their disorder.

Soften their glare.

Merge their dust.

This is called profound unification.

It cannot be achieved by attachment.

Neither can it be achieved by detachment.

It cannot be achieved by benefit.

Neither can it be achieved by harm.

It cannot be achieved by admiration.

Also, it cannot be achieved by contempt.

Therefore, the world admires it.

57 Ruling

以正治国
以奇用兵
以无事取天下
吾何以知天下其然也
才

夫天下多忌讳
而民弥贫
民多利器
而邦家滋昏
人多知
而奇物滋起
法物滋章
而盗多有

57

Use justice when ruling the State.
Use surprise when employing armies.
Use no effort when taking the world.
How do I know it is like this?
Only after this.

The more prohibitions there are in the world,
the poorer the people will be.
The more sharp weapons people have,
the more the State's household will be confused.
The more people know,
the stranger the things they begin to develop.
Rules increase the content of the law
and, therefore, there will be more criminals.

是以圣人之言曰
我无为也
而民自化
我好静
而民自正
我无事
而民自富
我欲无欲
而民自朴

Hence, the saying of the sages states:

"I practice Non-action

and the people will transform themselves.

I am tranquil

and the people will perfect themselves.

I use no effort

and the people will become wealthy by themselves.

I desire not to desire

and the people will become simple by themselves."

58 Ruling

其正闵闵
其民
屯屯
其正察察
其民
缺缺祸

祸福之所伏
福祸之所伏
孰知其极
其无正也
正复为奇
善复为妖
人之迷也其日固久矣

58

If the laws are very lax,

then the people will have

extreme surpluses.

If the laws are very strict,

then the people will have

extreme shortages and misfortune.

Misfortune is fortune's place to hide.

Fortune is misfortune's place to hide.

Who knows their extremes?

There is no normal.

Normal turns around and becomes abnormal.

Good turns around and becomes evil.

That has confused everybody for a long time.

是以圣人
妨而不割
廉而不刺
直而不绁
光而不耀

Therefore, sages are
interfering but not cutting,
sharp but not stabbing,
straight but not rigid,
and bright but not dazzling.

59 Frugality

治人事天
莫若啬
夫唯啬
是谓早服

早服是谓
重积德
重积德
则无不克
无不克
则莫知其极
莫知其极
可以有国

有国之母
可以长久
是谓
深根固氐
长生久视之道也

59

In ruling people and working with nature
there is nothing like frugality.
Only those who are frugal
are called to early service.

Prepare for the call to serve early
by a significant accumulation of virtue.
If there is a significant accumulation of virtue,
then nothing is impossible.
If nothing is impossible,
then one's limits are unknown.
If one's limits are unknown,
then one may possess the country.

Possess the Mother of the country
and accordingly endure long.
That is called:
having deep roots and a strong foundation.
Having a long life through a lasting regard for the Way.

60 Ruling

治大国
若亨小鲜

以道莅天下
其鬼不神
非其鬼不神也
其神不伤人也
非其神不伤人也

圣人亦弗伤人也
夫两不相伤
故德交归焉

60

Ruling a large country
is like enjoying small delicacies.

Use the Way to attend to the world,
then spirits will have no power.
It is not that spirits have no power,
but their power will not harm people.
Not that power cannot harm people.

Sages do not harm people either.
Both do not harm each other.
Therefore, virtue unites and returns.

61 Position

大国者天下之下流也
天下之交也
天下之牝也

牝恒以静
胜牡
以其静也
故宜为下也

故大国
以下小国
则取小国
小国以
下大国
则取于大国

故或
下以取
或
下而取

61

A large country should take a low position.
It is the intersection of the world.
It is the female of the world.

The female always uses tranquillity
to overcome the male.
She is tranquil.
Therefore, she is better in a low position.

Hence, a large country should
use a lower position than a small country,
when associating with that smaller country.
A small country should
use a lower position than a large country,
when associating with that larger country.

Therefore, some might take
the lower position to associate.
Others might be in
the lower position to associate.

故大国者
不过欲兼畜人
小国者
不过欲入事人
夫皆得其欲
故大
者宜为下

Those in a large country

only desire to merge and raise people.

Those in a small country

only desire to join other business people.

They all obtain what they desire.

Therefore, the larger one

better acts as the lowest one.

62 Success

道者万物之注也
善人之保也
不善人之所保也
美言可以市
尊行可以贺人

人之不善也
何弃之有
故立天子
置三卿
虽有共之璧
以先四马
不善坐
而进此

古之所以
贵此道者何也
不谓
求以得
有罪以免与
故为天下贵

62

People and All-things concentrate on the Way.
It is the protection for competent people.
It is the sanctuary for incompetent people.
Pleasing words might be exchanged.
Respectful conduct might honour people.

Incompetent people
forsake their existence unnecessarily.
Therefore, when the Emperor is crowned
and the three ministers are installed,
a mill-stone of jade
preceded by four horses,
is not as good as sitting down
and presenting this.

So, why did the Ancients
value the protection of this Way?
Did they not say:
*"Use it to obtain what you seek
and use it to escape what you suffer."*
Therefore, it is valuable for the whole world.

63 Non-action

为无为
事无事
味无味
大小多少
报怨以德
图难乎于其易
为大乎于其细也

天下之难
作于易
天下之大
作于细
是以圣人终不为大
故能成其大

夫轻诺
必寡信
多易
必多难
是以圣人猷难之
故终于无难矣

63

Act with Non-action.

Work without effort.

Taste without savouring.

Make the large small and the many few.

Repay hatred with kindness.

Pursue the difficult, while it is easy.

Act large, while it is still small.

The world's most difficult things

arise from the most easy ones.

The world's largest things

arise from the smallest ones.

Therefore, all sages will avoid great actions.

Hence, they can achieve greatness.

Those who make rash promises

are certainly difficult to trust.

Those who regard everything as easy

will have certainly many difficulties.

Therefore, sages regard everything as difficult.

Hence, they have no difficulties in the end.

64 Proactivity

其安也易持也
其未兆也易谋也
其脆也易破也
其微也易散也
为之于其未有也
治之于其未乱也

合抱之木
作于毫末
九成之台
作于蔂土
百仞之高
始于足下

为之者败之
执之者失之
是以圣人无为也
故无败也
无执也
故无失也

64

That what is at rest is easy to hold.

That what is not manifest is easy to plan.

That what is fragile is easy to break.

That what is small is easy to scatter.

Act when it has not happened yet.

Control it when it is not chaotic yet.

A tree that takes both arms to embrace

grows from a little cutting.

Nine-tenth of a tower

rises from a simple basket of earth.

A thousand meters height

starts from under your feet.

Those who act will fail.

Those who hold will lose.

Therefore, sages will use Non-action.

Therefore, they will not fail.

They will not hold.

Therefore, they will not lose.

民之从事也
恒于其几成事也而败之
故慎终若始
则无败事矣

是以圣人欲不欲
而不贵难得之货
学不学
而复众人之所过
圣人能辅万物之自然
而弗敢为

In handling their affairs,

people fail often close to their success.

Therefore, be as careful at the end as at the beginning.

Then affairs will not fail.

Therefore, sages desire not to desire

and do not admire goods that are difficult to obtain.

They learn not to learn

and repair the mistakes of others.

Sages complement the nature of all All-things,

but they do not dare to act.

65 Ancients

古之故曰
为道者非以明民也
将以愚之也
民之难治也
以其知也
故以知治邦
邦之贼也
以不知治邦
邦之德也

恒知此两者
亦稽式也
恒知稽式
是谓玄德
玄德深矣
远矣与物反矣
乃至大顺

65

Therefore, the Ancients said:

"Do not use the Way to enlighten people."

Instead, use it to keep them simple.

People are difficult to rule

if they use their knowledge.

Therefore, using knowledge to rule the country

is betraying the country.

Using no knowledge to rule the country

is benefiting the country.

Remember always those two things.

Examine also the principle.

Always remembering to examine the principle

is called profound virtue.

Profound virtue is deep.

Even far away things return to it.

The great order is perfect.

66 Position

江海之
所以能为百浴王者
以其善下之也
是以能
为百浴王

是以圣人之欲上民也
必以身下之
其欲先民也
必以其身后之

故其居上
而民弗重也
其居前
而民弗害也

天下皆乐
推而弗厌也
非以其无争也
故天下莫能与之争

66

How are the river and the sea
able to be the Kings of a hundred valleys?
They use competently their low position.
Therefore, they are able
to be Kings of a hundred valleys.

Therefore, sages who desire to be above the people
must place themselves below them.
Those who desire to lead people
must place themselves behind them.

Therefore, they stay above
and the people will not weight them down.
They stay in front
and the people will not harm them.

Everyone in the world will be happy
to elect them without objection.
Having no purpose, they do not strive.
Therefore the world cannot strive with them.

67 Treasures

天下皆谓我大
大而不肖
夫唯不肖故能大
若肖矣
其细矣

我恒有三宝
持而保之
一曰慈
二曰俭
三曰不敢为天下先

夫慈故能勇
俭故能广
不敢为天下先
故能为成事长

67

Everyone in the world calls me great.
Great and different.
Only those who are different can be great.
If they were similar,
then they would be insignificant.

I have always three treasures
that I keep and protect.
The first one is called compassion.
The second one is called frugality.
The third one is called humbleness.

Those who are compassionate can be courageous.
Those who are frugal can be generous.
Those who do not dare to act as the first of the world
can be successful leaders of affairs.

今舍其慈
且勇
舍其俭
且广
舍其后
且先
则必死矣

夫慈以战则胜
以守则固
天将救之
如以慈垣之

Now, those who abandon compassion

and are yet courageous;

abandon their frugality

and are yet generous;

abandon their humbleness

and are yet leading;

they will certainly die.

Those who use compassion to attack will triumph.

Those who use it to defend will stand firm.

Nature will protect them

with a wall of compassion.

68 Striving

善为士者不武也
善单者不怒
善胜敌者弗与
善用人者为下

是谓不争之德
是谓用人
是谓配天
古之极也

68

Competent warriors do not like war.

Competent chiefs will not get angry.

Competent conquerors will not engage.

Competent leaders will take a low position.

That is called the virtue of not striving.

That is called employing people.

That is called matching with nature.

It is the ultimate principle of the Ancients.

69 Resistance

用兵有言曰
吾不敢为主而为客
吾不敢进寸而退尺

是谓行无行
攘无臂
乃无敌矣
执无兵

祸莫大于无敌
无敌
近丧吾宝矣
故抗兵相若
则哀者胜矣

69

Warriors have a saying that states:
"I do not dare to act as a host, but act as a guest.
I do not dare to advance an inch, but retreat a foot."

That is called: moving without moving.
Rolling up the sleeves without showing an arm.
Be without resistance.
Hold without weapons.

No greater misfortune than meeting no resistance.
Meeting no resistance
is close to losing my treasures.
Therefore, when equal armies face each other
the reluctant one will win.

70 Lao Zi

吾言什易知也
什易行也
而人莫之能知也
而莫之能行也
夫言有宗
事有君
夫唯无知也
是以不我知

知我者希则我贵矣[5]

--- --- --- --- --- --- --- ---

是以圣人被褐
而裹玉

---

[5] This line is divided in the English text.

70

My words are very easy to understand
and very easy to apply.
Yet, people cannot understand them
and they cannot apply them.
My words have precedence
and my affairs have a sovereign,
but they do not understand that.
Therefore, they do not understand me.

I am valuable
to those few who understand me.
Therefore, sages wear cheap cloth
and conceal jade.

71 Weakness

知不知尚矣
不知不知病矣
是以圣人之不病也
以其病病也
是以不病

71

Knowing that you do not know earns respect.

Not knowing that you do not know is a weakness.

Therefore, sages are not weak.

They consider their weakness as a weakness.

Hence, it is not a weakness.

72 Ruling

民之不畏威
则大威将至矣
毋狎其所居
毋厌其所生
夫唯弗厌
是以不厌

是以圣人自知
而不自见也
自爱
而不自贵也
故去彼而取此

72

When people do not fear authority,
then greater authority will appear.
Do not take their dwellings by force.
Do not reject them a place to live.
Only, if they are not rejected,
then they will not reject you.

Therefore, sages know themselves,
but do not display themselves.
They love themselves,
but do not admire themselves.
Therefore, reject that and accept this.

73 Courage

勇于敢者则杀
勇于不敢者则活
此两者
或利
或害

天之所亚
孰知其故
天之道不争
而善胜
不言而善应
不召而自来
单而善谋
天网恢恢
疏而不失

73

Those who are courageous in daring will be killed.

Those who are courageous in not daring will live.

Those two things

could be beneficial

or could be harmful.

Nature takes a low place.

Who knows its reason?

The Way of nature is not to strive,

but to overcome through competence.

Without speaking, it answers with competence.

Without calling, things come.

It is simple and plans with competence.

The net of nature is very extensive.

It dredges and nothing escapes.

74 Ruling

若民恒且不畏死
若何以杀惧之也
若民恒畏死而为畸者
吾将得执而杀之夫孰敢矣

若民恒且必畏死
则恒有
司杀者

夫代
司杀者
杀是代
大匠斲也
夫代
大匠斲者
则希有不
伤其手矣

74

If people never fear death,
how could the use of executions scare them?
If people always fear death and act abnormal,
how could I dare to seize, hold, and execute them?

If people always fear certain death,
then there is always someone
in charge of executing them.

Those who act on behalf of the one
that is in charge of the executions,
execute as if they act on behalf
of the Master Carpenter.
From those who act on behalf
of the Master Carpenter
only a few will not
cut their hands.

75 Ruling

人之饥也
以其上食税之多也
是以饥
百姓之不治者也
以其上之有以为也
是以不治
民之轻死也
以其求生之厚也
是以轻死

夫唯无以生为者
是贤于贵生也

75

People are hungry,

because their food taxes are high.

Therefore, they are hungry.

Common people cannot be governed,

because their leaders act for their own purposes.

Therefore, the people cannot be governed.

People take death lightly,

because they seek to live substantially.

Therefore, they take death lightly.

Only those who do not act for the purpose of living

are knowledgeable at valuing life.

76 Strength

人之生也柔弱
其死也坚强
万物草木之
生也柔脆
其死也枯槁

故曰坚强
者死之徒也
柔弱
生之徒也

是以兵强则不胜
木强则折
故强大
居下
柔弱
居上

76

People are born soft and weak.

They die, hard and strong.

All-things, grasses, and trees

are born soft and fragile.

They die, dry and brittle.

Therefore, the hard and strong

are called companions of death.

The soft and weak

are the companions of life.

Hence, a strong army will not win.

A strong tree will be broken.

Therefore, the strong and big

occupy the low positions.

The soft and weak

occupy the high positions.

77 The Two Ways

天之道
其犹张弓者也
高者抑之
下者举之

有余者损之
不足者与之
故天之道
损有余
而补不足

人之道则不然
损不足
而奉有余
夫孰能有余
奉不足于天下者乎[6]

--- --- --- --- --- --- --- ---
唯有道者乎

---

[6] This line is divided in the English text.

77

The Way of nature
is like flexing a bow.
High things are lowered.
Low things are raised.

It takes from those who have plenty.
It gives to those who have not enough.
Therefore, it is the Way of nature
to take from what is plenty
and give to what is not enough.

However, the Way of people is different.
They take from what is not enough
and give to what is plenty.
Hence, those who have plenty
and give to those in the world
who have not enough
are the only ones who possess the Way.

是以圣人为
而弗恃
成功
而弗居也
其不欲
见贤也

Therefore, sages act,
but do not rely on it.
They succeed,
but do not claim.
They do not desire
to display their knowledge.

78 Humility

天下莫柔弱于水
而攻坚强者
莫之能胜也
以其无以易之也

故柔之胜刚也
弱之胜强也
天下莫弗知也
而莫能行也

故圣人之言云
受邦之垢
是谓社稷之主
受邦之不祥
是谓天下之王

正言若反

78

Nothing in the world is as soft and weak as water.

Yet, in attacking hard and strong things,

nothing has a greater ability to overcome them.

Therefore, nothing could replace its purpose.

The softest will overcome the hardest.

The weakest will overcome the strongest.

Nobody in the world does not know this.

Yet, nobody does practise it.

Therefore, sages have a saying that states:

"Accept the country's shame

and be called the Kingdom's leader.

Accept the country's misfortune

and be called the world's King."

True words seem to be paradoxical.

79 Justice

和大怨必有余怨
焉可以为善

是以圣人执右契
而不以责于人
故有德司契
无德司彻

夫天道无亲
恒与善人

79

Calm a great hate and certainly some hate will remain.
How could this be considered competent?

Therefore, sages adhere to orthodox agreements
and do not obligate other people by purpose.
Therefore, those with virtue will uphold the agreement.
Those without virtue will uphold the details.

The Way of nature has no favourites.
It is always with the competent people.

80 Ruling

小邦寡民
使有十百人之器
而毋用也
使民重死
而不远徙

有车无所乘之
有甲兵无所陈之
使人复结绳而用之
甘其食美其服
乐其俗安其居

邻邦
相望
鸡狗之声相闻
民至老死
不相往来

80

In a small country with a few people,
let everybody have many tools,
but not use them.
Let the people be serious about death
and not move far away.

Let them have carriages without using them.
Let them have weapons without displaying them.
Let them return to knotted cords and use them.
Sweeten their food and beautify their clothes.
Enjoy their customs and secure their dwellings.

Neighbouring countries
will see each other in the distance.
They hear each other's chickens and dogs.
Nevertheless, the people die of old age
and have never visited each other.

81 The Two Ways

信言不美
美言不信

知者不博
博者不知
善者不多
多者不善

圣人无积
既以为人
己俞有
既以予人矣
己俞多

故天之道
利而不害
人之道
为而弗争

81

True words are not pleasing.

Pleasing words are not true.

Those who know are not educated.

Those who are educated do not know.

Those who are competent have not much.

Those who have much are not competent.

Sages do not hoard.

Since they are used to act for other people,

they receive more possessions for themselves.

Since they are used to give to other people,

they have much more themselves.

Therefore, the Way of nature

is beneficial and without harm.

Accordingly, the Way of people

should be action without strive.

Notes

Discussion

Congratulations, you have completed the first step of your 2,500 years journey back to the eternal wisdom of ancient China. You have almost reached your destiny.

Almost—because *Lao Zi's Dao De Jing* contains still hidden layers of poetic beauty, wisdom, and knowledge. The aim of my book *Lao Zi's Dao De Jing: Meta-translation (Schade, 2016)*[7] was to create a reliable English version for the book that you are reading right now. Whether my attempt was successful or not, there are still many levels of understanding hidden within Lao Zi's manuscript. No matter how reliable, no translation is sufficient for an adequate understanding of Lao Zi. Even Chinese people reading a pristine copy of his manuscript in their mother language, need to discover the eternal wisdom that lays buried deep below the surface of Lao Zi's poetic style and simple words. In accord, Lao Zi warned his readers—*My words are very easy to understand and very easy to apply. Yet, people cannot understand them and they cannot apply them (70)*. He also states that he does not intend to enlighten them—*Do not use the Way to enlighten people. Instead, use it to keep them simple. People are difficult to rule if they use their knowledge (65)*. Furthermore, he created confusion by using a poetic-holistic style and different poetic names for the same concepts such as—*The Way, Nothing, One, Father, Mother, Valley Spirit, etc.*

---

[7] Appendix: Lao Zi Meta-translation

This suggests that *Lao Zi's Dao De Jing* is an esoteric manuscript that contains hidden knowledge about the *Way of Nature* and the *Way of People*.

To add to the confusion, *Lao Zi's Dao De Jing: Chinese-English Dictionary (Schade, 2017)*[8] shows that each Chinese pictograph has many meanings. The actual meaning of each pictograph is determined by its context, which is Lao Zi's sophisticated philosophy. In order to understand *Dao De Jing*, one needs to know the core of Lao Zi's philosophy. For two and halve thousand years, thousands of scholars around the world have tried to discover that key. Despite their great efforts, it remained hidden behind the poetic veil of Lao Zi's misleading simplicity.

My study suggests that the core of Lao Zi's brilliant philosophy is his sentence—*The One generated the Two (42).* That has been the guiding principle for the explanations in my book—*Lao Zi's Dao De Jing Explained (Schade, 2017).*[9] The ancient *Ma Wang Dui* texts are the most pristine versions of *Dao De Jing* available, because they were buried in an undisturbed tomb for over two thousand years. Intriguingly, compared to those texts, that crucial line was moved in later versions. That displacement of one single sentence increased the elusiveness of Lao Zi's manuscript significantly. Was this

---

[8] Appendix: Lao Zi Dictionary
[9] Appendix: Lao Zi Explained.

done to clarify the text, or alternatively, to hide the knowledge of a civilization that Lao Zi called the *'Ancients'*?

Think Smarter with Nemonik Thinking (Schade, 2016)[10] is the operating manual for your mind that you should have received at birth. Nemonik thinking is a smarter way of thinking that aims to maximize your success by evaluating seventeen nemoniks, which are memorized keywords describing all the perceived aspects of the mind, reality, and their interaction. In terms of Lao Zi's philosophy—*Success is to obtain what you seek and escape what you suffer (62).* You might be the smartest thinker in the world, but only nemonik thinking could make you the smartest thinker you can be. Lao Zi's *Dao De Jing* is important for nemonik thinking, because it provides a rationale. In addition, it provides the eternal wisdom that is required to make productive decisions about each of the 17 nemoniks. Therefore, the nemonik template is used to reorganize Lao Zi's manuscript for *Lao Zi's Dao De Jing for Nemonik Thinkers (Schade, 2016).*[11]

---

[10] Appendix: Nemonik Thinking
[11] Appendix: Lao Zi for Nemonik Thinkers.

Appendices

Bibliography

Schade, A. (2016). *Lao Tzu's Tao Te Ching* (1 ed.). nemonik-thinking.org.

Schade, A. (2016). *Lao Zi's Dao De Jing for Nemonik Thinkers* (1 ed.).

Schade, A. (2016). *Lao Zi's Dao De Jing: Meta-translation* (1 ed.). nemonik-thinking.org.

Schade, A. (2016). *Think Smarter with Nemonik Thinking*. nemonik-thinking.org.

Schade, A. (planned 2017). *Lao Zi's Dao De Jing Explained* (1 ed.). nemonik-thinking.org.

Schade, A. (planned 2017). *Lao Zi's Dao De Jing: Chinese-English Dictionary* (1 ed.). nemonik-thinking.org.

Schade, A. (planned 2017). *Sun Zi's The Art of War* (1 ed.). nemonik-thinking.org.

Schade, A. (planned 2017). *The Unreal Reality* (1 ed.). nemonik-thinking.org.

Index

My Other Books

Lao Zi's Dao De Jing

Lao Zi's Dao De Jing (Schade, 2016).

This book comprises synchronised Chinese and English versions of *Dao De Jing,* which means—*The Way of Nature and the Way of People.* Lao Zi was a Chinese philosopher who lived during the 6th century BC but is still ahead of our time. His brilliance outshines intellectual giants such as Confucius, Sun Zi, Socrates, Plato, and Aristotle. Lao Zi's aim is to teach success, which is to *obtain what you seek and escape what you suffer.* Success is achieved by aligning the *Way of People* with the *Way of Nature.* Lao Zi's success is secular and based on competence, rather than devotion. It is about positioning, rather than competing. Lao Zi's deep understanding of nature and people is crucial for your immediate survival and that of the next generation. We are facing overpopulation, dwindling resources, nuclear warfare, pollution, climate change, etc. We cannot solve those problems with the same way of thinking that is causing them. The brutal reality shows that our way of thinking is failing. Therefore, Lao Zi's eternal wisdom is the guiding light for our future. Its simplicity reaches peacefully across the boundaries of race, religion, spiritualism, ideology, and science.

Lao Zi Meta-translation

Lao Zi's Dao De Jing: Meta-translation (Schade, 2016).

Lao Zi's eternal wisdom shines through in the numerous English translations of his *Dao De Jing*. Nevertheless, comparisons show that some individual Chinese pictographs and their interpretations are unclear. Therefore, this meta-translation is based on seven reputable Chinese versions. In order to select the most reliable pictographs, each one was compared across all versions. As changes might have occurred over time, the chance of a pictograph being included depended on the age of the version in which it appears. The consistent use of each pictograph was enhanced by computer assisted comparisons across the entire text. In addition, ten reputable English translations were synthesized in order to extract an initial context for each pictograph. The selected pictographs were translated with *Lao Zi's Dao De Jing: Chinese-English Dictionary (Schade, 2016)* that was compiled for this purpose. The guiding principle for this meta-translation has been the core of Lao Zi's philosophy—*The One generated the Two*. The importance of that sentence is explained in *Lao Zi's Dao De Jing Explained (Schade, 2017)*.

Lao Zi Explained

Lao Zi's Dao De Jing Explained (Schade, planned 2017).

For more than two and a half thousand years, *Dao De Jing* has been shrouded in mystery. The poetic beauty of Lao Zi's words has maintained its dazzling shine that hides his esoteric secrets. In accord, Lao Zi wrote—*My words are very easy to understand and very easy to apply. Yet, people cannot understand them and they cannot apply them.* Many scholars have attempted unsuccessfully to peel away layer after layer of meaning to unravel its cryptic secrets. In contrast, the present book reveals Lao Zi's secret teachings for the first time in a clearly understandable way, imparting hidden knowledge about the *Way of Nature* and the *Way of People*. The core of Lao Zi's teachings is success, which is—*obtaining what you seek and escaping what you suffer.* Success is secular and based on competence, rather than devotion. It is about positioning, rather than competing. It is achieved by aligning the *Way of People* with the *Way of Nature*. The guiding principle for the present explanation is the core of Lao Zi's philosophy—*The One generated the Two.* Humanity is facing huge manmade problems with a failing way of thinking. Therefore, Lao Zi's eternal wisdom is more relevant than ever.

Lao Zi for Nemonik Thinkers

Lao Zi's Dao De Jing for Nemonik Thinkers (Schade, 2016).

Lao Zi's Dao De Jing: Meta-translation (Schade, 2016) provides a reliable Chinese-English translation. Nevertheless, *Dao De Jing* has no rational sequence comprising an introduction, main body, and discussion. Even the division of the manuscript in the parts *Dao* and *De* is ambiguous. Topics concerning the *Way of Nature* and the *Way of People* appear almost ad random in the parts *Dao* and *De*. Similar to the notation *Jing*, the division in *Dao* and *De* might have been added later. Lao Zi's unfamiliar format suggests that he used a holistic, rather than a rational approach. He seems to walk around the topic, while telling the reader what he is seeing from different angles. Although that approach enhances the mystery and poetic beauty of that amazing manuscript, it did not produce the most efficient teaching tool. Therefore, I have used the nemonik template to restructure *Dao De Jing* for nemonik thinkers. This template was introduced in *Think Smarter with Nemonik Thinking (Schade, 2016)*.

Download a free eBook version
@ nemonik-thinking.org

Lao Zi Dictionary

Lao Zi's Dao De Jing: Chinese-English Dictionary (Schade, 2017).

Lao Zi's manuscript is more than 2,500 years old, while most Chinese-English dictionaries focus on the modern meaning of Chinese pictographs. Therefore, this special dictionary was compiled from several reputable public resources in order to get as close to the true meaning of each pictograph as possible. *Lao Zi's Dao De Jing: Meta-translation (Schade, 2016)* is based on seven Chinese versions of *Dao De Jing.* Altogether, those versions comprise about 1,600 different pictographs, which are included in the present dictionary. Furthermore, this dictionary introduces a unique numerical coding system for Chinese pictographs that could improve the search method concerning hard copies of Chinese reference books.

Download a free eBook version

@ nemonik-thinking.org

Nemonik Thinking

Think Smarter with Nemonik Thinking (Schade, 2016).

This is the operating manual for your mind that you should have received at birth. Nemonik thinking is a smarter way of thinking that aims to maximize your success by evaluating seventeen nemoniks, which are memorized keywords describing all the perceived aspects of your mind, reality, and their interaction. Success is obtaining what you seek and escaping what you suffer. To maximize that success, nemonik thinking mobilizes the hidden genius, accelerates thinking, improves memory, reveals opportunities and threats, creates questions and ideas, and reduces stress levels. It is like playing a musical keyboard with seventeen keys producing an infinite repertoire of smart strategies. Nemonik thinking is unique because it is the first exhaustive and transferable way of thinking. In contrast, conventional thinking is time consuming. Hence, the less time you have, the greater the necessity to study nemonik thinking. You might be the smartest thinker in the world, but only nemonik thinking could make you the smartest thinker you can be.

Download a free eBook version
@ nemonik-thinking.org

Nemonik Glossary

Glossary of Nemonik Thinking (Schade, 2016).

Nemonik thinking is a competitive advantage because it mobilizes the hidden genius, accelerates thinking, improves memory, prevents blind-spots, and reveals opportunities, while its constant preparedness reduces stress levels. Definitions, associated with the mind and reality, are inherently hypothetical, fuzzy, and intertwined. Nevertheless, to improve our understanding of the way we think, we have to identify, differentiate, and define those components. Therefore, this glossary provides descriptions for the concepts associated with nemonik thinking. To become skilled in nemonik thinking, it is recommended to study— *Think Smarter with Nemonik Thinking (Schade, 2016).*

Download a free eBook version
@ nemonik-thinking.org

Nemonik Dictionary

Dictionary Nemonik Thinking (Schade 2016).

Nemonik thinking mobilizes the hidden genius, accelerates thinking, improves memory, reveals opportunities and threats, creates questions and ideas, and reduces stress levels. Nemonik thinking divides the mind into 17 nemonik regions. That division defragments information, which facilitates the storage, maintenance, recall, and processing of associated information from memory. However, the boundaries of the nemonik regions are fuzzy. Therefore, the aim of this dictionary is to differentiate them by providing keywords for each nemonik concept. The first part of this dictionary translates nemonik concepts into common keywords e.g. *advance* into attack, bypass, etc. In contrast, the second part translates common keywords into nemonik concepts e.g. attack, bypass, etc. into *advance*. This dictionary shows that the complexity of conventional thinking comprises thousands of keywords that can be simplified to 17 nemoniks. This reduction will increase the speed of your thinking. To become skilled in nemonik thinking, it is recommended to study—*Think Smarter with Nemonik Thinking (Schade, 2016).*

Education Kills Humanity

Education Kills Humanity (Schade, 2016).

Humanity is facing huge manmade problems such as overpopulation, dwindling resources, pollution, climate change, and warfare. Nevertheless, we should not blame corrupt politicians, uncaring industrialists, greedy investors, passionate greenies, and warmongers. They are the products of our educational system, which conditions students with ratings to maximize the probability of winning. Winning is defeating opponents in competition. Therefore, conventional thinking is conflict oriented, which fosters aggression, control, effort, and force. This inhibits the truth and, therefore, it is self-destructive. The educational failure is maintained by cognitive dissonance and groupthink. In contrast, nemonik thinking aims for success, which is to obtain what you seek and to escape what you suffer. Therefore, nemonik thinking is goal oriented, which fosters freedom, alignment, compassion, allies, and win-win strategies. You might be the smartest thinker in the world, but only nemonik thinking could make you the smartest thinker you can be. This manuscript is an abridged version of *Think Smarter with Nemonik Thinking (Schade, 2016).*

Global Warming

Global Warming is the Solution (Schade, 2016).

This book presents a bilateral hypothesis for climate change. Mainstream climatology lacks scientific integrity and statistical methodology. Peer review is changed into peer pressure and objectors are silenced by labelling them *'Deniers'*. Proper statistical analyses are replaced by fancy graphs and non-causal correlation analyses. The conclusions are predominantly based on the last 166 years, while 420,000 years of Antarctic data are ignored. Climatology also ignores the solar expert Professor Zharkova, who predicts a mini ice-age by 2030. The present study shows that the current 400 ppm of CO_2 predicts a global temperature of 11.5 °C. It also shows that the observed global temperature of 1.3 °C failed to reach statistical significance. In addition, the data support the hypothesis that we live in a glacial period. This hypothesis is supported by the thermal gap of CO_2, the long interglacial duration, and the interglacial thermal stability. Consequently, decreasing atmospheric CO_2 could induce glacial conditions threatening the survival of humanity.

Download a free eBook version
@ nemonik-thinking.org

Sun Zi's The Art of War

Sun Zi's The Art of War (Schade, planned 2017).

Sun Zi (554-496 BC) was a Chinese warrior-philosopher who wrote the military classic *Bing Fa* or *The Art of War*. Although his book is about war, his strategies apply to every facet of daily life. Sun Zi deals with the art of positioning yourself in space, matter, and time. He addresses the questions raised by nemonik thinking of where, what, and when to advance, stay, retreat, accumulate, preserve, dispose, act, wait, prepare, accept, reject, reveal, and conceal. Think smarter and incorporate Sun Zi's strategies in your thinking. To become skilled in nemonik thinking, it is recommended to study—*Think Smarter with Nemonik Thinking (Schade, 2016).*

Download a free eBook version
@ nemonik-thinking.org

Website

It is the aim of my website to provide interactive on-line information about nemonik thinking. This includes discussions, books, blog, videos, exercises, updates, activities, web links, and tests. Join the nemonik thinkers and receive the latest updates. It is a work in progress. Check it out and have your say! I look forward to your feedback at:

nemonik-thinking.org